Asylum in the Grasslands

Asylum in the Grasslands

Poems by Diane Glancy

The University of Arizona Press
Tucson

The University of Arizona Press
© 2007 by Diane Glancy

Library of Congress Cataloging-in-Publication Data
Glancy, Diane.
Asylum in the grasslands : poems / by Diane Glancy.
p. cm.
ISBN-13: 978-0-8165-2571-3 (pbk. : acid-free paper)
ISBN-10: 0-8165-2571-4 (pbk. : acid-free paper)
1. Great Plains—Poetry. I. Title.
PS3557.L294A89 2007
811'.54—dc22
                    2006009132

Publication of this book is made possible in part by
the proceeds of a permanent endowment created with
the assistance of a Challenge Grant from the National
Endowment for the Humanities, a federal agency.

Manufactured in the United States of America on acid-
free, archival-quality paper.

12   11   10   09   08   07   6 5 4 3 2 1

Contents

Asylum in the Grasslands

If I were to tell a story

about a trip I had taken, I would talk about other things. They
would not seem relevant. If I talked about a trip, it would not
be that particular trip, but I would go back to the first trip the
sun took out of the Great Spirit's hands. You know how at first
it was burning everything up, and the Great Spirit had to let it
go. He had to let it move around so all the sky beings, the stars
and planets, the little dogs of the moons, would follow. And
in their flying they would cool. Then I would talk about other
places. And the relationship between trips. I would talk about
who was there, what caused us to go to those particular places.
How we each saw them in our own way. I would go into the
history of tribal migration. How we start out someplace other
than where we are. I would talk about the ancestors. How they
followed a stick from the west. Long ago they walked east and
then down the coast to the southeast. Then west again during
removal. By then you would be telling me to get on with it. I
would talk about my concept of history. *My* side of the whole
thing. And I would talk about the nature of talk. You would not
have patience or time. I would talk about reciprocity as a general
principle. It would not be quick. I would make up a story for
the story of my trip. I would say, we can get even this off the
ground.

The Artificial Indian

Because I could look straight through
my hands I could see
the bones
there was nothing I could hold
not even treaty lands
because the heavens rolled back
the sun nearly burned off my hair
because I did not know how to back off
because I could not shade my head
I waved at nothing
I came knocking into the spirit world
a tumbleweed
a ghost
an emptiness made full of fire.

Buffalo Medicine

I want to speak buffalo.

It was a day for honor. The herd walked the Great Plains. This way the herd walked. That. The little band of Indians followed. How they depended upon us. How we clothed their bodies. Fed their stomachs. Provided hides for their teepees. We often spoke to them. Grunting in language they understood. There was nothing we didn't give. But now we take our grasslands. Our lawn chairs and yard goods. Stampede to the other world. From the council-fire of heaven we are called. The Great Spirit speaks in soldiers' guns. From trains, they pass shooting.

Surely America was made for us. Remember how often we delighted them. Deciding how we would run through the prairie with the wind in our ears. Our large heads pure with mind. The Great Spirit great as he spoke. Yo. We were his. We grunted his praises. Snorted and roamed in his will. Our calves grew up in our strength. We were kings. We allowed death. We gave ourselves for the Indians.

We are called Grandmother buffalo. *Señor búfalo. Mon duc buffle. Herr bürgermeister büffel.* Savior buffalo. Universal buffalo. Surely the Great Spirit was made in our image. Touch us and you see the face of God. Our heads are angels fallen to the prairies. Touch us and you hear the grunting God.

Surely the angels sing our grass-eating song. Ho ee yo. The clouds rumble over us. The wind-currents follow. The whole earth sings to us earth-movers. The prairie highways remember our migrations. Put our feet on four little wheels. Roll us on the knolly prairie. The creosote roadbeds black as our nose. The grass once tall as our backs.

Almost

1

Before the Little Big Horn
the Grandmothers had a vision of Cheyenne

2

falling upside down.
More than had ever been this distance

1

which is nearly life. Later
the winter brush,

2

the windows tall as trees
whose ideas almost form in the head.

1

Whose hands not under the cover
of skin all ghost-like

2

in the fields. Ah this place.
No, that. *Kay no tos.*

1

The plans nearly catch this time.
The duck-decoy Custer.

2

A snap of metal-
detectors in a shooting gallery.

The Cherokee as Light Fragments Reflected from the West Window I Remember at the Old House

Light broken by the trees / the curtain closed on us to sleep
for the afternoon / I couldn't sleep / but struggled against the
white wall / the hole of the mouth the words come from / *amnal*
/ *burraflo* / I tried to speak / the longing to get up / leave the
room / ride into the afternoon between lines of combed fields /
the furrowed runways / I watched the sun travel like the old car
/ the dusty road / the afternoon I tried to back out of my bones
/ water popping in the radiator when I stopped / the steaming
hole of the hose into the engine spouting / the furious gurgle if
I got out of bed / a flock of birds roaming the wall / the Indian
tribes forced to sleep / their language following light from the
curtained room.

Boarding School for Indian Women

1

Pulling up a piece of mud, it spreads on the water. Now land swims, not knowing what it is, not having what takes the not knowing.

Bureau chests, iron beds. The linen girls wash in the boarding school. On the wall, Christ on a stick, his popgun lifted at us.

I turn the pages of the book. We sleep with this Christ nailed over our beds. This leaning, walking-stick Christ, close as a nail in a hand.

2

The long white room sometimes is a garden. The bean flowers, the sun chirping on the floor. We had old migrations across the land.

I hate to hold what was, but it sits on my lap. There are times, even with Christ I am not happy.

The crickets in the garden rows are our mud lodges by the river. Yesterday the groundskeeper mowed the cornstalks, the withered bits of stubble. A few bodies of squash in the rows after the raid.

3

We study the Bible in a classroom. Jael, the wife of Heber,
nailed the head of Sisera to the floor when he slept.

I think how the women dismembered soldiers. Pale squash in
the garden without arms or legs.

But when we study Christ punctured, his blood ran out and we
are healed.

We accept this piece of mud we pulled up from water. The white
man and more of him coming.

After the class, we think Christ makes soldiers whole again. We
cry in our sleep.

Among the stubs of cornstalks in the garden, the umbilical
charm of a young snake.

4

Strikes-Two and Hand-Shakes give legs back to our tales. Under
the Bible stories, their voices before the light of this new world.

I listen to them at the tub where we stir sheets. In the
washroom, shadows cross the floor, climb the wall like
hollyhocks in the garden.

5

Across the road, a house, a white barn, a chicken house, a shed.
We stand at the fence and look.

Once we had another world, but it got crowded and we pulled this mud nest from water. Now our world is taken, and we are left with this shadow of our making.

The next world is far away.

We feel our hulls sifted like grain. We hoe sheep manure into the turnips and beets.

A white butterfly in the grape arbor, the row of sheets on the line. Spring house, rock shed. All that would run from us.

Sister Mary Eustella Cruzievska, 1887–1938

Nun's Cemetery, Our Lady of the Lake Convent, San Antonio

Not a prayer book of shade.
We rolled up the top layer of our skirts
and dug the grave.
The shovel of Sister Mary Majella Podlewska,
Mary Polycarpe Cenka,
like the tongue of God.

We tied back our wimples.
No one sees us but the mesquites.
Their hairy arms twist over the walk.

She suffered at the last
to be with her husband.
Her suffering came in waves.
Nothing to wake the mouth. She recited
what she'd lived without.
A smell of red chilies in the black beans,
the yellow of squash and pears.
Voices she remembered before she left
on the train from Pittsburgh.

Nothing of our own.
Hush, Mary Clotilda.
Sister Mary Edonxia.

Dig the grave
for Sister Mary Eustella Cruzievska.
Our habits heavy in the heat.
The bugs around our heads
like little black electric fans
of the priests.

Fodder

Forgive our trezpasses against us
like a lean-to / we no knot whad we due.
The arrows of missiles / lazer beamies
open the eyeball of the urth.
Druzzle the wigwam.
Wheezing chilerns.
Tutal cumz to tell uz how to read
theze blocks of letters.
Boz. Wheebut. Iz wuz nerd ezy.
We god to laughing.
Hernry my brother
ezpecially garfooned at the table.
Here iz ours /
the storehouse / sheds / all the fieldstones
of our taking breath /
the wurds that make our farms
and iz the animals that urnhabit them.
Az whad wurds uz, Tutal saz, angry at our laf.
Seeze the room.
Sneeze iz ours. Achoom.
Who bring it? Great Spirid vacoom.
Sounds running oud our mouth and noz.
Meaning out of eyez.
Chief Jezus dominion bee yurz.
Yeur wurds baffaloing the medicine men.
Yeur holy wurds.

Manger still gruzzling animals.
Put away hauze / cattle / gupe / geraf
zereba with stripes / camuel.
My wicket spirit buzzards yeur wurds / Tutal.
White star in a tree.

The Great Divide

The spirits of the ancestors migrate. They drink the last lick of yellow light from the creek. I hear them like wind in the cornstalks. One ancestor always shakes his knee with restlessness. A hole torn in his moccasin for a sore toe. I tell him I have the hollowness of this air. I have to live this life I don't like. I have to go where he doesn't count. I say to the ancestors, you only call me back. In the squeak of brakes I hear your ceremonial whistle. In the blink of neon I see your fires. Wait for me in the back booth at the all-night cafe. Leave your pony-drag at the coatrack. Shuffle your feet when I come in and I'll know you're there.

Wajeema

Wajeema, third wife of Hitoowah, or Corn Nose, wrapped her
blanket around her. The dark night rattled her head. She heard
the tar-paper shack flapping in the storm like a frightened crow.
She wasn't going to leave Hitoowah, though he didn't want
her. Already he thought of his fourth wife. Wajeema cooked
fry bread, chopped off the head of the hen he stole from the
chicken farm. In her blanket, Wajeema thought of the bar in
Wallow, Nebraska, with one lightbulb hanging down where
Hitoowah drank. She could almost see the whiskey-soaked
light. The barren prairie was wide as the backseat of Hitoowah's
DeSoto where Wajeema rode wrapped in blankets when he
brought her to his place. Now she burrowed in the bed, holding
nothing. Hitoowah's first and second wives were back with
their mothers. But Wajeema wasn't leaving. She hid her head
in the dark. She couldn't return to her mother. The house was
full of children with more coming. She would stay in the night
that circled her head. She rubbed her eyes. The nothing sparked
tiny white stars that twirled in back of her eyes. She drove
lodgepoles into that place in her head. She constructed hides.
Yes, she was going to stay. Wajeema would tie herself to the
lodgepoles, going over each movement in her head. Now she
heard the car. Maybe it was some of Hitoowah's older children
returning as they did now and then. Maybe it was Hitoowah
with another wife. He would throw Wajeema from his house
in the storm. She held the thought of the teepee, her heart
pounding the lodgepoles.

Indian Summer

There's a farm auction up the road.
Wind has its bid in for the leaves.
Already bugs flurry the headlights
between cornfields at night.
If this world were permanent,
I could dance full as the squaw dress
on the clothesline.
I would not see winter
in the square of white yard-light on the wall.
But something tugs at me.
The world is at a loss and I am part of it
migrating daily.
Everything is up for grabs
like a box of farm tools broken open.
I hear the spirits often in the garden
and along the shore of corn.
I know this place is not mine.
I hear them up the road again.
This world is a horizon, an open sea.
Behind the house, the white iceberg of the barn.

Meatloaf

Now Great-grandmother comes through the backdoor. Her head latticed like corncribs, her legs tied with chicken wire. Her limbs had been taken quickly apart, bones dismantled, spirit folded up. She moves around the room. Come, I put my hand on the table. She sits in a chair. Her eyes are blown out by solar winds. I have heard the breath in her throat when I scraped the rake across the bare yard. Two fingers on her hands rattle like winter leaves on the tree. Words hiss through her head. *Do-ga-ske-v-se-gu-hanaugh*. I shrug in frustration. How do I tell her even the words of her Cherokee language do not survive? I put her hand to my head, but she takes it away. She is not deaf or blind! I see her buckskin gnawed by the teeth of wolves. Her feet trail bits of a comet. I put the drip-pan under her. Something like grease spots the floor. Her heart simmers from the long trip, and I hear it sputter as she cools. For a moment she seems to forget where she is, and I hold a piece of bread to her nose. I pass her my plate of meatloaf. She puts the napkin on her lap and prays. *Wo-no-gah-le-sd*. She lifts the teacup with her two fingers. I watch her eat. Soon I point to the vast plains of space at the end of my porch. She makes a circle with her thumb and two fingers. Even the universe is round, and I nod that I've heard it's so. I wonder what turn she missed to get here. I see my thought reaches her. She only stopped for a visit, grabbing what she could to wear. Otherwise she'd be invisible to the eyes I have in my head, the little bowls of lard. *Pssnah!* She spits, then sweeps crumbs from the table. I watch the buffalo cross her cheek. Under the buckskin there are grapevines for her rib cage. In her pocket a map of pit stops on the large arc of her restless migration.

I Hear a Medicine Man

His ghost churrs the walls of my house. He speaks to me of
folding up the quilts on my unmade bed. Of packing the car
and taking my cat north. *Hey tonka.* He sits on a white horse,
black hail-spots on its hips, streaks of lightning down its legs.
He stands in the living room with my sofa and rocks. *Hey tonka.*
He calls. Split-tail swallows circle the ceiling. *Two leggeds / four
leggeds / wings of the air. Pack.* Arrows point northward on the
road marked with bison hooves. The white cleansing road. The
sacred blizzard winds of endurance. And my sore cat, who used
to run through the yard and climb trees and call to me to show
me where she was, now bit on the rump by a cat who stalked
her, stays in the house. *Pack*, she says. These are hard winters
when we are hounded by soldiers again and know hunger. The
medicine man stands at the door. Bison horns on his head,
white geese feathers in his braids. His horse neighs. The earth
is old and not well. Pass through the land of bison slaughter
and the square, dirt-roofed reservation houses. The graves of
our grandfathers, their wives and children. Do not cry. We are
another wave migrating to the grasslands of the next world.

Portraits of the American West

Alfred Jacob Miller, El Paso Museum of Art

First of all you find an acorn.
Or the squirrel.
Perhaps something you hold from the past
beyond memory
into heritage
or ancestral levels of thought
and you're following the long haul
of old heat fueled on campfires.

It's somewhat disappointing after a while.
This guy's still in the direction of the sunset
overrimmed with too much of a nineteenth-century eye.
I mean
Indians holding their ears
and the title, *Waiting for the Locomotive*.

The curly hairs of buffalo,
horses
all too arabesque and harem-like
could be more of a caravan to Egypt, yes
biblical.
There's Joseph on a camel
just sold

like a treaty.

Landscape of Light

1

He is thinking
nothing can matter.

All the light
rays through scrub

oaks on the
low afternoon focus

into one hole
in the clouds.

His father killed
by a fall

from a horse.
His mother and

sister standing in
the yard. Nothing

ahead that he
can see. Not

like families whose
ways are set

from childhood. No,
disruption was his

inheritance. A jumbling
of roads not

here, or there,
maybe not anywhere.

2

My father never
said how he

left, and I,
riding in the

sack of his
testicles, have no

memory. He worked
in the packing

house. All day
the cattle going

their forfeited way
while we with

life wander the
wilderness. Nothing left

but each day
starting new with

nothing. A jar
of bread-and-butter pickles

from his mother
on the table.

All generations as
though the first.

Wondering where to
go, what to

do. The same
effort of scattered

light to find
the focal point

in the clouds.
This vast sensation

of sun making
a rickety crop

in the field,
of which there's

not much left,
nothing at all

when his father
died. And he

with his mother
and sister to

support while others
were far on

their own way.
He must have

felt the light
fall apart each

day. His mouth
open under the

sky with the
web of nerve

endings that meet
and give direction.

The net of
lines under scrub

oaks that touch
and hold together,

not unthreading the
lives of each.

3

But he knew
he would break

even as the
sunlight hits the

clouds, falls through,
scrambles back from

different places on
the earth, trying

to get into
the sky, Holy

Father, and us
with him in

Christ's blood. We
have to make

a land before
we can see

a way through
it, build highways

and toll gates.
But for now

he talks sweetly
to the animals

as they climb
the chute, enter

the kill. His
wife and children

in the yard.
Each looking up

for the light.
How many generations

have passed in
this darkness, and

we have yet
to find the

chute that makes
the family rise?

4

Once the bottomland
was campground by

the river. My
father feels whatever

tribes were there
when soldiers rode

near. Children quiet,
the women hum

their prayer song.
Then the knives

and arrows. Afterward
the squaws cut

the legs off
soldiers so they

can't return from
the next world.

Then somewhere a
settler suspends a

cabin from the
ground. He plows

the sun across
the bottomland. Then

a farmer in
the roll of

light above the
river builds his

pastures. Builds a
pecan grove for

his wife, nailing
up each tree

under the sky
until it takes

root. The dark
soil dumped from

heaven where the
pecan grove casts

its shadow like
a net. The

knot of teepees
and campfires forgotten

in the row
of trees. Now

the city near.
The pecan grove

torn down for
stockyards, cutting trees

like the legs
off soldiers, taking

animals from their
pens, sending them

to the next
world. Now my

father hears the
church bell on

the river bluff
above the stockyards.

Maybe he is
thinking it matters

after all. The
years of struggle

under the broken
light. The continuity

of dark after
which something happens.

5

Is it hope
or faith, a

gift from the
Spirit? My father

is in an
attitude of prayer.

For the first
time his mouth

opens in praise.
Ekk cay may.

The Spirit fills
my father. His

feet in the
stockyards, his head

through the clouds.
Now my father

speaks. Is it
after death we

have this inheritance,
finally, from God?

We rise to
comfort the river.

The endless war-cries
lifted in the

late evening fog.
O EE OOOO.

6

Maybe later my
father scoops the

moon like a
bucket of black-walnut

ice cream. In
his eyes the

Indian tribes gather.
There's a multitude

of lightning bugs
in their campfires.

Hey cah may.
My father chants.

Now he is
thinking he has

come far. His
mother in the

grave, his sister
married. Children taller

than the white
picket fence. Without

knowing it, he
breaks the spell,

has something to
pass onto others

who start over
again. In his

head I see
thoughts fuse. Suddenly

there is MEMORY!
There is light

breaking on the
ground soon to

rise to the
clouds through the

tunnel of the
past. And we

are left with
a MAP! A

past! From his
bed he feels

the soldiers, the
struggling generations. He

gives his light
back to the

clouds like a
turnpike-ticket when he

passes. I take
the flashlight of

sun on the
low afternoon in

the riverbottoms, read
the map he left.

Yes, here, maybe
there. The whole

earth rises through
the scrub oaks.

We walk on
air and never

know it. No,
from the first

we are strangers,
pilgrims. We are

all this light
scrambling for return.

Hershel

Now it's my father
starting his trip
from the hospital ward,
declining curtains
on a roll, and we
are together who were
at odds on the eve
of allowances.
The old wound of a car
in the drive.
It was so much and it
was nothing. The ever-
lasting pain of it.
But now we're together
who have been miles
away, and I wish for
another tongue,
another past to build
the moment on.
One last chance before
he falls into the
ground. The drizzle
of irises on his table.
The nothing I can
give him while he
lingers in the hollow

passage of the throat.
Words sprout rootless
as the place closes down.
Arms and lungs.
The heart and toes.
The fork in the road
that can't be turned
back from. His car
sideways, there's someone
running, telling him
he can't turn around.
They're motioning
he has to follow
to its end. I know it
as I stand with him.
The words in his eyes,
black fishing holes
he'd give anything
to get back to.
But tubes tie him
to the dock. The shoes,
houses he shined
with paint. Each day
he belongs less to me.
The small black grip
of his heart searching
the dark ceiling
for a passage. It's a
lesson I received each
day like thirty lashes.
Yet at times he would
have given me anything.

And I want to say,
suddenly, stay for
one more piece
of chocolate cake.
You know, the icing
the woman next door
taught me to make.
The toss of water, little
flops of it on the shore.
The wobbly ramp you
step onto, not
sure it's fastened down.

The Funeral

All these lovely people
gathered around the pine trees,
gone for some time now,
they are back to lift us from this life
when it is time.
Oh I know it's so.
My grandmother told me
her husband was in the hall before she died,
and my grandfather had been dead for years.
And I stood at my father's bed before he died.
It was his mother with him
and a group of spirits I didn't recognize.
Their gathering bigger than ours
under this little canopy in the rain.
Distance is no measure.
They can be here sooner from farther away
than I who came from Oklahoma.
You can't get ahead of them.
They are here with their knowing smiles,
the way marked in their hand.

Amelia's Breakfast

An idea happens
you know it all your life

your mother grows old
first a kidney

then a spot on the liver
even prayers won't cover the starlings at dusk

you hear them on the chimney
a single-engine plane missing

somewhere life flies to it
a puzzle the child works in a world

you still try to fit together
but locate her sudden movements

Grand Junction where you turn left
you know she stays in bed most of the day

a gift you unwrap
don't want

and don't know why you're getting it
put it to your nose

the goggles for your eyes
all night her feet peddle the rudders

the scarf a runway from her neck
now she leaves the door open

who used to lock everything up
the plane somewhere clearing the trees

up over fields
back to the piano lessons before she met

your father she dreamed of on the farm
dashed back to the ground

you never know what happened
the engine stalled over fields

her hand a falling-leaf pattern
arms flapping

you sit beside her bed and wonder
where she is now

the single-engine in her suitcase
a day's underwear when you visit

though you hope this time she is Houdini
and can get out of it

you see her mouth move and lean closer
you guess her speechless words

say the hereafter is no worse
than exhaust

behind a delivery truck
when your car stalls in traffic

you drive all that way
while she makes shapes with her mouth

asking for dolls or babies
she left miles back

ideas the body can't follow
the cat like damp wool

when it comes in out of the rain
the smell of her closed-up apartment

a cold paw on your knee
toast and Ovaltine in the morning

her arms spread like a parachute
her fingers the tips of the plane's wings

not even leaving a flare to let you know
where she is

anger that your son comes in
in the middle of the night

you can't sleep again for the engine roar
spitting oil

the body stretched between bedrock and air
in the hollow that holds the ocean

your hand signals out the window
left turn to the infinite

where all math is understood without
the holes of space in your paper

where unknown answers orbit the aviatrix
falling slowly in the air.

Girl Who Won the Minnow

Chief Wahoo wanders after dark as though I were the papoose
he carried on his back. But I am with you, Mother, in your
death. We fish the quarry pond where miners ripped coal out of
the fields when you were a girl. You wander now with me back
to the farm as though I were a doll you had. The farmer's tractor
spurts after light shakes out its dust in the field. Now you coo
like pigeons on the chimney of your apartment. Your noise /
theirs / traffic / helicopter like your Mixmaster when you used
to beat up cakes. You slump in the chair, your robe opened. The
heat as though the oven door not closed. It lasts so long here,
well into fall, and we're still on the last coals of summer. When
I come back it is the same as when I left. The dominoes on the
table, the wax from all the floors you shaved with your mop.
Only to regret it now. Ribs of a crib stake the cemetery where
Wahoo is buried and you with him. Already death squats at your
chair. You almost pet it with a crate of relief. Your life scattered
as someone's notebook across the road when school lets out
for the summer. Now you curl in my arms, Mother, up through
the back roads of Kansas from Oklahoma to Missouri, that long
drive now three summers. Kidney removed, tumor scorched
with radiation. But it comes back on you / a small fish under
the dock nibbling the line / our shuffle step to your bed. It's
yours now. I drive the road sometimes in sleep over and over,
remembering how you taught me to fold my will like a quilt
and stuff it in the hall closet. You gave me a basket of cherries,
stems raised like hairs on my arms when the ghost of Wahoo

nears the quarry. I unfold the opportunity of the highway / the
tunity of God / morbid decline of the body / *cooing* / *cooping*
/ *coping*. Language is still enough. I lean into your face and
say, *There will be a light and you will follow it.* Others wait. Your
mother and father, your Wahoo chief husband, the sister who
died at birth, grown now like you. The rest of us later. You
gag at the sink. Squirm in bed as though at the quarry pond.
Something finally on the end of your hook.

Long Way Out

1

I feel like coming out of what bothers me.
Mother with cancer quiet as a baseball game,
volume down.

Once rain made a puppet show on windows,
now campfires flicker
a strange night game played in a shadow world
crackling with radio static.

2

Tribes of Plains Indians gather in the drive.
I listen to their voices in the dark rain.

Their grievances stir like traffic
on the interstate
I hear even in autumn with one window open.
They smolder like piles of leaves.
Their horses snort thunder.

In the yellow lightning,
I see their flares of cooking fires.

Hee aaahhh caayyy.
I hear their anger at postholes
by the north road.

It's where my daughter and I gathered leaves
on a brighter day,
cold in the shade, still hot in the sun.

But this October night,
horses fret the rained-out game,
ground soggy as a softball mitt.

I hold my hand over their noses.

Mother, we outlast the small, wet dugout
of the grave.

Home Cooking #29

Sometimes she knows me and calls
for me to get her up. *I can't,*
I say. She asks, *Why not?*
Her body's near its death.
She wants applesauce, calls
ones I can't remember.
She's busy in her house.
There's steam at the foot of her bed.
I tell her, *It's not steam.*
She says, *It is.* The muffins
just out of the oven, the oatmeal
hiccupping like a faucet drip
in the sink, the pink curtains
blowing the whole farmhouse.

Home Plate

I don't think much can hold us down.
You go shrieking and squirming into the
dugout. Your body's here, your mind
there, but you come out of it. I don't
know if it's Christian faith or what,
but the last weeks of her death
were bearable. And when we saw her
before the wake, she was beautiful.
There's a power that transcends horror.
Of course, I was not the one dying, but
I think she would say the same. If she could
unscrew the tin lid of heaven, she would
tell us it was like coming out of a warm-up
when it's your turn to bat.

Mother Good-bye

You were the watermelon slice on summer evenings. Your transparent teeth left a hole in our lives. Pudding and gristle. The sea the shape of a watermelon wedge. Sawtooth waves over half the slice. Under the ship, a spike from the base toward it like the old paper-spindle on your desk. Now the sea's a jar of black-cherry juice you bought. The ship punctured by the spike. The column of disease rips you from our hands. Cannot hold onto you. The grave, Mother, is a piece of mind chipped off the wedge.

Doll's Bones

I ask you, *what could I do?*
The bed in the corner with its
knobbed posts, the window that pulled open
from the wall, the bed stand with its lamp,
the trapped heat in summers,
the frigid cold in winters.
I stayed in that attic room,
hollow as the doll I played with
in the upstairs of the old house.
At night, a ghost sucked my feelings,
swallowed marrow and joint, the sinew
that once lifted one leg and the other
so I could descend and climb the stairs.
I felt I was the putty
my father put into the windows for winter.
I knew I could do nothing but shuffle
Sunday school papers,
read of Jesus and him crucified,
dead, and raised.
Maybe the outbursts of anger
were from being stifled each day.
The family closed within the walls.
Yet the decency of them kept me
when I was at the door.
I tell you,
the earth is not a place for comfort.

It takes a belief in doll's bones.
Over and over when you ask what holds me,
I say,
it is Christ,
it is Christ,
it is Christ.

He Opens and Closes the Store

Wears a cowboy duster. His hair is white. His eyes are flames.
A sword dashes from his mouth. When he speaks, his voice
has the sound of many waters: *I am he who lived and died and
live forever*. His bronze boots burned in a furnace. On the
shelves of his store: palm branches, sackcloth, harps, a box of
earthquakes, another box of numbers. Floods and a dragon. A
volume of wars entitled *For a While It Only Looked Like They Were
Ahead*. Four horses tied up out back. The store often thunders.
His names are *Lion of the Tribe of Judah, Root of David, Bright &
Morning Star*. On the counter, locust wings with the sound of
chariots and horses running to battle, though I think now they
are helicopters and planes. Vision of horses with heads of lions
and out of their mouths come fire and smoke. Sweet cannons
and missiles. A bowl of wrath. A bolt of linen. You can hear his
cowboy boots when he steps in the back room. You don't forget
this albino. I feather-dust his shelves when I know he's coming.
I bristle like a porcupine. *Precious Lamb*, I say. *Holy*. No other
words. He's stored gasoline for his locust machines. I know his
underground sights. I bale hay for his four horses ready to ride.
When he's in the store I seem to know all things. It's worth the
backseat wagon ride it took to get to his place. It's worth it to
be outsold a moment in history. Soon he cuts the linen into
handkerchiefs. He empties the bowl of wrath out back by the
horses and gives me the pilot helmet, which is a lion head. I put
my arms into the locust wings. *Giddyup*, he says. We fly to the
mountains upheaving and the sea washing over its coasts. The

dragon shoots his fire into the plains and it dries like cowhide.
The land thrown up and down in a rodeo. I put my fingers in
my ears because of the wailing and noise, put my fingers in my
nose over the plague of sores and swollen tongues. Stars fall
to earth like figs from a shaken tree. Hail. Fire and drought. I
hear an angel say, *Woe to them on earth*. It's the time when wings
lift and the nose points back down to earth. Death flees and
only the torture of furnace heat. War and more wars and even
I do not tell all. But this I will say, we were busy for years with
the handkerchiefs and handing out the long robes and sorting
through the rubble for ones who called his name. And when
it was over, we climbed in the hayloft over what used to be
Minnesota and twanged the guitars until after the millennium,
saying, *Glory and dominion and power*.

What the Mutt?

The animal did not know they were not one. His black, wet nose wedged in the attic door. Up there motes of dust stirred in the window's sunlight. Cobwebs moved. He heard the sputs of a trapped bird. What the spirit was, he was. You could not see the seam. He could take his fur and claws onto heaven's floor. But it was extreme up there. Aching in summer, terrifying in winter. The ages stored in boxes and chests and trunks. How he yapped at the backdoor away from the attic and scraps of cloth a quilt preserves. Outside, the terminal snow, the yellow wells of piss. *Hoida*, he hissed. The animal could run in the yard. Through him the spirit had paws. He chirped to the snow. The white starkness of it hurt his eyes. *Yosanna. Bark. Bark.* He ran in circles nearly blind from the light.

Chief Bemidji

Gustav Hirsch, 1898, Depot Museum, Bemidji, Minnesota

Wooden Indian
carved from a log
armless /
footless beneath his trouser leg.
Once his *ma'kizin,s* were moosehide
w/ cattail down for warmth
and beading
which are berries of the Great Spirit.
Once his arms.
Once his feet.
He was Shay-now-is-kuing
rattle or *one who makes a jingling sound*
renamed Bay-me-ji-ga-maug
a river (the Mississippi) *runs through the lake* (Bemidji).
Dimmest lightbulb.
Weathered masthead.
Hardly any features left
splitting
splintering
still facing the struggle of two worlds.

Exegesis

1. Two rakes lean against the brick house I don't know the names of. One with long fingers ready to play the piano. The other short and arthritic. 2. The days I wasn't traveling, the dog would bark across the street when the mailman came. The room with a hem that showed like the dress she let down. 3. I remember her dying and thinking, how do you come to the end of your life and not know where you're going? 4. Ironing the hot cotton. The sharp smell of the underarms from sweating knowing one day she'd come to this. 5. All those moorings laid one upon the other like flowers on her grave. Now she's beside my father again. He's hunting for quail. She's stewing she's left behind, knocking down my brother and me. Always reminding us we were the earth she's under. 6. Nothing more of the rakes. But the room: a) The written text on walls, b) the lines of the wood floor, c) the minute openings in the screen.

Catfish Fishing

1

Razorblades jump in your fist

2

Look at the spirit markings in his scales—
the eye-marks in his tail.
Hi yip, I would say—

1

bayonets float in your eyes

2

The fish is a friend like the buffalo.
Thank him for his life.
Let the fish come and eat with us.

1

as you explain with a jerk of your head

2

Set him a place at the table with finger bowls
he can stick his nose into
when he must suck water for breath.

1

how the hook must enter the lip or jaw

2

Let him hold his breath the rest of the time
like we hold ours when we are in his element.
Tie a bib around his fat neck.

1

or better yet how the fish swallows

2

Serve him insects in a silver chafing dish.
What lovely sleeves his fins make.
What stripes and speckles and spots along his dorsal!

1

and the hook catches in its gut—

2

Spear him quickly through the heart
while he thinks of his blessing from the Father.
While he thinks of the fine buckskin of his life

1

You slice him in two while he takes his first bite.

2

and his mouth still opens and closes like smoke signals
let loose in the wind that seem to say, Tula, Tula,
though I can't be sure it's quite that.

The Bowl of Judgments

1. Sometimes you go into yourself and stand at the chain-link fence. Your fingers grip the wires. Your nose pushed to a hole. 2. You look into the pupil of the black sky. You see dirt from roads you sifted with your father's car. You feel furnace heat rising under your dress. You think you will be there forever. 3. The checked bedspread patterns your face. Your arms and legs are bedposts. 4. Your mouth seems to count backward. Your tonsils snipped out. Bones powdered for fertilizer. Your fat rendered into lard. You never thought you'd come to this. 5. You sit up in the covers. You thump your head and feel the road lop under a flat tire. 6. Over your shoulder you see the stockyards across the 12th Street Viaduct in Kansas City, where you used to live. You even hear the church bell on the hill. It's where you know you've been when you come back to yourself, resolute and clear.

Returning on an Oklahoma Back Road Late at Night with 139,000 Miles on My Car

I think of the times I have driven across the prairie in wind
storms / I have spoken to the angels that ride on the fenders
/ one night there was a tapping sound in the engine and the
angel got out its wrench and reached through the hood while
I drove / they go through walls you know and it stopped that
noise because I couldn't be stranded on the road at night / I
could not live without the scaffolding of belief / the other world
plopped down over me like an old Indian blanket / I could not
survive the dark / the one angel wears a headband the other a
vest with patches of the states it's been in / saying *ki ye ki yip* to
the buffalo eyes of stars up over me in the night / I drive under
Christ my knees rattling like these dried cornstalks / I feel the
car lift off the road I know the angels flap their wings / the one I
think its name is Earl / the other I'm not sure / Jacob I suppose
/ the one who doesn't always watch the road but smells the
engine / wipes the temp-gauge / pokes the carburetor again /
bugs fly by with the wings of cherubim / the eyes all revved up
in the dark / that one bright star Jesus looking through the nail
hole in his hand.

Easement (or, Now Let It Rest)

Clytemnestra:
Go home quietly.
What has been, it had to be.
Scars enough we bear, now let us rest.
Agamemnon, Aeschylus

I remember once
when my husband's grandmother was visiting,
she said I could write
when the children were grown.
Meanwhile her grandson
marched off to his battle without waiting,
without hindrance other than what came
from within.
And surely it took all those years
I was under the lid of them, serving.
What did it matter?

I find a tube of snakeskin
by the lawn mower.
A brittle transparency opened at the head.
A crackly robe.
Delicate.
Royal.
Something the children
would have played with.
I turn it between my fingers.

The underneath has sections
like rows of books on a library shelf.
The top is cluttered with clear stones
tumbling to the sea.
This is where someone made a run for it,
someone leaped to the she-spring out there
in the field,
writhing between mower blade and the wall
of the shed as if to bongo and jazz.

Is it a robe Clytemnestra wore
after her daughter Iphigenia
was sacrificed so winds would lift the sails
to Troy?
Ugly Helen.
All for her.
Then the curly tongue of Clytemnestra
flicked.
The tip of her nose tore,
the delicate skin around the eyes.
The ripping throat.
She broke out of herself,
jumped in rose clumps
and the stunted nosegays of earth.
The screams of Iphigenia cackling in the ears
hidden in her head.
Sometime in the night her new self
slithered out glistering like quick
under a hangnail.

I roll the snakeskin in my hand.
I think of the sacrifice of women.
It's always been that way.
Maybe in the plan of it
someone has to tend the children,
cook,
wash,
and maybe I just couldn't do it all,
but those tender years
stayed under the transparency
like a sheet of plastic at a window
in winter.
Maybe I was safer there
than here where I wonder what will happen
without the shelter I once had,
the grandmother telling me
to put it all back in my head.

Asylum in the Grasslands

He commanded them to sit down on the grass
Mark 6:39

When some adjustment occurs
not in the actual circumstances
no they seem to stay the same
but in one's attitude
or way of viewing those circumstances

that other way into acceptance
or at least liveability
so one is not assumed to be in a lock
that can't be stepped beyond

it's a fragile gate
the opening of faith
the letting of anotherness into your shadow box

you know you'll feel a kind hand
somewhere in the middle of your back
it's not that you want to be relieved
of your burdens
it's what you're here for

but you meet someone in the prairie grass
his face so full of light he's milk-eyed

you let his ideas roll over you
you even forget the bitterness you learned
all your life
though you know there's a loveliness
in suffering
but you let go of it a little

you assume the air
walk over what was supposed to be your grave

you even feel it's the way it's supposed to be

this Savior who sucks you into himself
this man with his eyes in backwards.

Concerto for Piano and Orchestra

Aram Khachaturian, Tucson Symphony Orchestra

he talks to the white bones of the piano
I hear his breath-talk
as he plays the boning
of the huge black-fish piano

yubber
I sit under the moving gills
front row
the orchestra hall's a whole ocean
half-way through there's sea-mist
on his forehead

more wind
and the fiddles are flying fish
like birds they fly
saying *yaz we breathe air now*

air now
air

How to Explain Christ to the Unsaved

An awkward cousin who could not get a date, and you didn't
know anyone who would go out with him. Too dark and ruddy.
Too swarthy and crazy in the eye. He had a slow walk you could
outpace. He was someone you thought you could outrun. But
he could stop you dead with something he said. Or his voice
would break into thunder. He was—concerned. Preoccupied.
You remember Crazy Horse with his eye on the next world. His
horse with a mission, too. Not just holy but knowing how to
get down to it of late. No one else would come by or call, but
this man, who rode a donkey and would end up wearing a hat
of thorns, would stay with you. Who was this prophet, this
traveling man, this nomad born with animals? He was jovial as
a penitentiary. He became a grandfather spirit, and his believers
saw into the sky. He was too tall, too lanky. He was a loner.
Atonement was never a group act, but for the sheep and bulls
and rams, I suppose, over the burnt altars of old encampments.
But he was self-possessed. The soldiers nailed him to a cross. He
was in hell three days and brought out everyone who wanted to
enter his kingdom he had just named Heaven. Now he sleeps,
they taunt, but it may be the sleep Adam slept when a rib was
taken for you-know-who or whom, and if Christ sleeps, it is the
sleep while the cross is taken from him, called rib bone for a
bride.

Last of the Man Dog

Man Dog reliable
Man Dog heap
Man Dog boogles w/ big chief
You hear him at night,
his firelights so mixed
you hold a magnifying glass.
He's a tin cup,
snow shovel,
plow.
The pilgrims—was it settlers—
trying to figure,
still split beyond repair.
It was said
to be a ghost
or wholly in this world.
A lot going on.
What you choose
as you intermix—
Whew, this hard,
this riveted box,
the buckboard.
Whoa, horse.

Acknowledgments

Acknowledgment to *Michigan Quarterly Review* for "Buffalo Medicine" and "Meatloaf"; *Sulfur* for "Mother Good-bye"; *Feminist Studies* for "Fodder"; *Seneca Review* for "Boarding School for Indian Women"; *Turtle Quarterly* for "Boarding School for Indian Women," "I Hear a Medicine Man," and "The Funeral"; *Callaloo* for "If I were to tell a story" and "I Hear a Medicine Man"; *Artful Dodge* for "Amelia's Breakfast"; *howling mantra* for "Returning on an Oklahoma Back Road Late at Night"; *The Journal* for "Concerto for Piano and Orchestra"; *Blue Pitcher* for "Almost"; *The Phoenix* for "Landscape of Light" and "What the Mutt?"; *Gin Mill* for "Long Way Out" and "Home Cooking #29"; *In-Print* for "Girl Who Won the Minnow"; *Sheba Review* for "Catfish Fishing"; *Husk* for "Exegesis"; *Swamp Root* for "The Bowl of Judgments"; *North Dakota Quarterly* for "The Great Divide"; *Night Sun* for "Indian Summer"; *Pivot* for "Hershel"; *World Literature Today* for "The Artificial Indian," "Wajeema," and "The Cherokee as Light Fragments"; and *Image* for "How to Explain Christ to the Unsaved."

I thank *Iowa Woman* for their award to "He Opens and Closes the Store."

I thank the Poetry Society of America for the *Writer Magazine*/Emily Dickinson Award to "Sister Mary Eustella Cruzievska."

I thank *Abiko Quarterly* for their award to "Easement (or, Now Let It Rest)." "Doll's Bones" also appears in that journal.

Acknowledgment to *The Sacred Place*, edited by Scott Olsen and Scott Cairns, University of Utah Press, for "Asylum in the Grasslands" and "*Portrait of the American West.*"

"Buffalo Medicine," "If I were to tell a story," "Boarding School for Indian Women," "Meatloaf," "Asylum in the Grasslands," "He Opens and Closes the Store," "Fodder," and "Returning on an Oklahoma Back Road Late at Night" are included in *Rooms, New and Selected Poems*, Salt Publishers, Cambridge, 2005.

I also thank the Minnesota State Arts Board for making this manuscript possible.

About the Author

Diane Glancy is a professor at Macalester College in St. Paul, Minnesota, where she has taught Native American literature and creative writing. She is currently on a four-year sabbatical/early retirement program. In 2005, Glancy wrote a play from her latest book, *Stone Heart*, a novel of Sacajawea, the young Shoshoni woman who accompanied Lewis and Clark on their 1804–1806 expedition. The play, *Stone Heart: Everybody Loves a Journey West*, was presented at the Autry National Center in Los Angeles in February and March 2006. Her latest collection of poems, *Rooms, New and Selected Poems*, was published in 2005 by Salt Publishers, Cambridge, England. A collection of her stories about the late nineteenth-century Ghost Dance, *The Dance Partner*, was published by Michigan State University in 2005.